MUM'S
WIT AND WISDOM

QUIPS AND QUOTES FOR MARVELLOUS MOTHERS

RICHARD BENSON

MUM'S WIT AND WISDOM

This edition copyright © Summersdale Publishers Ltd, 2018
First published as *Mum's Wit* in 2010

Illustrations © RetroClipArt/Shutterstock.com

Summersdale Publishers Ltd
46 West Street
Chichester
West Sussex
PO19 1RP
UK

www.summersdale.com

Printed and bound in Poland

ISBN: 978-1-78685-060-7

Substantial discounts on bulk quantities of Summersdale books are available to corporations, professional associations and other organisations. For details contact general enquiries: telephone: +44 (0) 1243 771107 or email: enquiries@summersdale.com.

Disclaimer
Every effort has been made to attribute the quotations in this collection to the correct source. Should there be any omissions or errors in this respect we apologise and shall be pleased to make the appropriate acknowledgements in any future edition.

CONTENTS

EDITOR'S NOTE

As William Makepeace Thackeray once said, 'Mother is the name for God in the lips and hearts of little children.' And your children are the apple of your eye. From baby's first steps to holding your first grandchild, motherhood provides a lifetime of magical moments.

But don't let these little cherubs fool you; they're your one-way ticket to the wonderful world of nappies, sleepless nights and back-chat. From one hair-raising moment to the next, they will rattle your nerves and turn your home upside down. And then there's adolescence.

So when you no longer give a pram and you're ready to throw out the bassinet with the baby in it, sit back and enjoy these hilarious quips and quotes, and remember why being a mum is the best job in the world.

WHAT IS MOTHERHOOD?

NOTHING BEATS HAVING THIS BEAUTIFUL CHILD LOOK AT ME AND SAY, 'MUM'.

Nicole Appleton

Never being number one in your list of priorities and not minding at all.

JASMINE GUINNESS

It's the biggest on-the-job training programme in existence today.

ERMA BOMBECK

Mothers… speak the same tongue. A mother in Manchuria could converse with a mother in Nebraska and never miss a word.

WILL ROGERS

I understood once I held a baby
in my arms, why some people…
keep having them.

SPALDING GRAY

It is to decide forever to have your
heart go walking around outside
your body.

ELIZABETH STONE

A mother's happiness is like a
beacon, lighting up the future but
reflected also on the past in the
guise of fond memories.

HONORÉ DE BALZAC

Nothing will ever make you as happy or sad, as proud or as tired.

Elia Parsons

It intensifies who you are, but also forces you to stretch and go beyond anything you thought possible.

FELICITY HUFFMAN

I want to make a better world… that's motherhood.

CASS ELLIOT

In our law books… Mother was believed to have been so basic that no definition was deemed necessary.

MARIANNE O. BATTANI

Pride is one of the seven deadly sins; but it cannot be the pride of a mother in her children, for that is a compound of two cardinal virtues – faith and hope.

CHARLES DICKENS

Motherhood is perhaps the only unpaid position where failure to show up can result in arrest.

MARY KAY BLAKELY

Maybe a little overprotective. Like I would never let the kid out – of my body.

WENDY LIEBMAN ON WHAT KIND OF MOTHER SHE WOULD BE

HAVING SOMEONE ELSE TO BLAME WHEN THERE IS A RUDE SMELL IN THE AIR.

Jane Horrocks

A TWINKLE
IN THE EYE

I rely on my personality
for birth control.

Liz Winston

Familiarity breeds contempt –
and children.

MARK TWAIN

Sometimes when I look at all my
children, I say to myself, 'Lillian, you
should have stayed a virgin.'

LILLIAN CARTER

There's a time when you have to
explain to… children why they're
born, and it's a marvellous thing if
you know… by then.

HAZEL SCOTT

Women who miscalculate
are called mothers.

ABIGAIL VAN BUREN

NEXT TIME I'M NOT JUST HAVING
AN EPIDURAL FOR THE BIRTH — I'M
HAVING ONE FOR THE CONCEPTION.

Sally James

I LIKE TRYING TO GET PREGNANT. I'M NOT SO SURE ABOUT CHILDBIRTH.

George Eliot

A WOMB
WITH A
VIEW

If pregnancy were a
book they would cut out
the last two chapters.

Nora Ephron

I studied pregnancy symptoms –
moody, big bosoms, irritable.
I've obviously been pregnant
for twenty years.

VICTORIA WOOD

Life is tough enough without having
someone kick you from the inside.

RITA RUDNER

Typical of Margaret. She produced
twins and avoided the necessity of
a second pregnancy.

DENIS THATCHER

Being slightly paranoid is like
being slightly pregnant – it tends
to get worse.

MOLLY IVINS

I feel cheated never being able to
know what it's like to get pregnant.

DUSTIN HOFFMAN

The only time a woman wishes she
were a year older is when she is
expecting a baby.

MARY MARSH

BEING PREGNANT IS AN OCCUPATIONAL HAZARD OF BEING A WIFE.

Queen Victoria

Carrying a baby is the most rewarding experience a woman can enjoy.

JAYNE MANSFIELD

Every four weeks I go up a bra size… it's worth being pregnant just for the breasts.

NATASHA HAMILTON

I've got seven kids. The three words you hear most around my house are 'hello', 'goodbye', and 'I'm pregnant'.

DEAN MARTIN

HAPPY
BIRTH-DAY

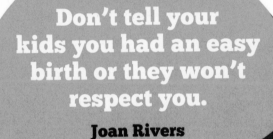

Don't tell your kids you had an easy birth or they won't respect you.

Joan Rivers

A suburban mother's role is to deliver children obstetrically once, and by car for ever after.

PETER DE VRIES

[THEY] NEGLECT TO TEACH ONE CRITICAL SKILL: HOW TO BREATHE, COUNT AND SWEAR ALL AT THE SAME TIME.

Linda Fiterman on antenatal classes

Speech-making is exactly like
childbirth. You are so glad
to get it over with.

JOHN BARRYMORE

There is a power that comes to
women when they give birth.

SHERYL FELDMAN

Although present on the occasion,
I have no clear recollection of the
events leading up to it.

WINSTON CHURCHILL ON HIS OWN BIRTH

HAVING A BABY IS LIKE TRYING TO PUSH A GRAND PIANO THROUGH A TRANSOM.

Alice Roosevelt Longworth

A woman has two smiles that an angel might envy: the smile that accepts a lover before words are uttered, and the smile that lights on the first born babe, and assures it of a mother's love.

THOMAS C. HALIBURTON

I wanted to give birth as opposed to being delivered.

RICKI LAKE

Just thinking about the pain makes me want to take drugs.

ELLEN DEGENERES

A little like watching a wet St Bernard
coming in through the cat door.

JEFF FOXWORTHY ON CHILDBIRTH

I'm not interested in being Wonder
Woman in the delivery room.
Give me drugs.

MADONNA

These wretched babies don't
come until they are ready.

QUEEN ELIZABETH II

Ladies are requested not to have children at the bar.

Sign in a Norwegian bar

Giving birth is like taking your lower lip and forcing it over your head.

CAROL BURNETT

WHEN I WAS GIVING BIRTH THE NURSE ASKED, 'STILL THINK BLONDES HAVE MORE FUN?'

Joan Rivers

I think of birth as the search
for a larger apartment.

RITA MAE BROWN

FOR WHEN A CHILD IS BORN THE
MOTHER ALSO IS BORN AGAIN.

Gilbert Parker

IF MEN HAD TO HAVE BABIES, THEY WOULD ONLY EVER HAVE ONE.

Diana, Princess of Wales

I GOT YOU, BABE

Here we have a baby.
It is composed of a bald
head and a pair of lungs.

Eugene Field

Babies are born looking like
the ugliest relative on his
side of the family.

JENNY ECLAIR

The worst feature of a new baby
is its mother's singing.

KIN HUBBARD

I can't think why mothers love them.
All babies do is leak at both ends.

DOUGLAS FEAVER

When I was born I was so ugly the doctor slapped my mother.

RODNEY DANGERFIELD

I think my life began with waking up and loving my mother's face.

GEORGE ELIOT

If you desire to drain to the dregs the fullest cup of scorn and hatred that a fellow human being can pour out for you, let a young mother hear you call dear baby 'it'.

JEROME K. JEROME

BEGIN, BABY BOY, TO RECOGNISE YOUR MOTHER WITH A SMILE.

Virgil

The hand that rocks the cradle
usually is attached to someone who
isn't getting enough sleep.

JOHN FIEBIG

It's extraordinary to look into a
baby's face and see a piece of
your flesh and your spirit.

LIAM NEESON

Loving a baby is a circular business…
The more you give the more you get.

PENELOPE LEACH

Up until they go to school, they're
relatively portable.

LIZ HURLEY

A baby is a loud noise at one end,
and no sense of responsibility
at the other.

RONALD KNOX

'Diaper' backwards spells 'repaid'.
Think about it.

MARSHALL McLUHAN

People who say they sleep like a baby usually don't have one.

Leo J. Burke

BOTTLING
IT

Reasons for breastfeeding: the milk is
always at the right temperature;
it comes in attractive containers;
and the cat can't get it.

IRENA CHALMERS

Breastfeeding should not be
attempted by fathers with hairy
chests, they… make the baby sneeze.

MIKE HARDING

A babe at the breast is as much
pleasure as the bearing is pain.

MARION ZIMMER BRADLEY

Breastfeeding is a mother's
gift to herself, her baby
and the earth.

PAMELA K. WIGGINS

THE BABE AT FIRST FEEDS UPON
THE MOTHER'S BOSOM, BUT IS
ALWAYS ON HER HEART.

Henry Ward Beecher

An ounce of breast milk is even more potent than the finest tequila.

Tori Amos

KIDDING
AROUND

The fundamental job of a toddler is to rule the universe.

Lawrence Kutner

Even when freshly washed and
relieved of all obvious confections,
children tend to be sticky.

FRAN LEBOWITZ

I think children shouldn't
be seen or heard.

JO BRAND

There is only one pretty child
in the world, and every
mother has it.

PROVERB

I am scared easily; here is a list of
my adrenaline-production:
1. Small children…

ALFRED HITCHCOCK

Any kid will run any errand for you
if you ask at bedtime.

RED SKELTON

There never was a child so lovely,
but his mother was glad
to get him asleep.

RALPH WALDO EMERSON

My mother loved
children – she would
have given anything
if I had been one.

Groucho Marx

A child is a curly dimpled lunatic.

RALPH WALDO EMERSON

THERE IS NO RECIPROCITY. MEN LOVE
WOMEN, WOMEN LOVE CHILDREN.
CHILDREN LOVE HAMSTERS.

Alice Thomas Ellis

Parents learn a lot from their children about coping with life.

MURIEL SPARK

It goes without saying that you should never have more children than you have car windows.

ERMA BOMBECK

Instead of needing lots of children, we need high-quality children.

MARGARET MEAD

MAD ABOUT THE BOY

The only time a woman really succeeds in changing a man is when he's a baby.

Natalie Wood

If that's the world's
smartest man, God help us.

LUCILLE FEYNMAN, AFTER *OMNI* MAGAZINE NAMED
HER SON RICHARD THE WORLD'S SMARTEST MAN

There was never a great man
who had not a great mother.

OLIVE SCHREINER

A man loves his sweetheart the most,
his wife the best, but his mother
the longest.

PROVERB

A boy's best friend is his mother.

JOSEPH STEFANO

The one thing a lawyer won't
question is the legitimacy
of his mother.

W. C. FIELDS

Few misfortunes can befall
a boy which bring worse
consequences than to have a
really affectionate mother.

W. SOMERSET MAUGHAM

OF ALL THE ANIMALS, THE BOY IS THE MOST UNMANAGEABLE.

Plato

All women become like their mothers.
That is their tragedy. No man does.
That's his.

OSCAR WILDE

But I never bump and grind… I'd
never do anything vulgar before
an audience. My mother would
never allow it.

ELVIS PRESLEY

A brief season of exhilarating liberty
between control by their mothers
and control by their wives.

CAMILLE PAGLIA ON THE ADOLESCENCE
OF TEENAGE BOYS

It takes one woman twenty years to make a man of her son – and another woman twenty minutes to make a fool of him.

HELEN ROWLAND

Happy is the son whose faith in his mother remains unchallenged.

LOUISA MAY ALCOTT

Boys will be boys. And even that wouldn't matter if only we could prevent girls from being girls.

ANNE FRANK

Well behaved: he always speaks as if his mother might be listening.

Mason Cooley

DARLING
DAUGHTERS

A DAUGHTER IS A BUNDLE
OF FIRSTS THAT EXCITE
AND DELIGHT.

Barbara Cage

To me, luxury is to be at home with my daughter; and the occasional massage doesn't hurt.

OLIVIA NEWTON JOHN

A fluent tongue is the only thing a mother don't [sic] like her daughter to resemble her in.

RICHARD BRINSLEY SHERIDAN

I was a mum so late in life; my daughter was the greatest thing since sliced bread.

CANDICE BERGEN

She named the infant 'Pearl', as being of great price – purchased with all she had – her mother's only treasure!

NATHANIEL HAWTHORNE

MY PARENTS TREATED ME LIKE I HAD A BRAIN – WHICH, IN TURN, CAUSED ME TO HAVE ONE.

Diane Lane

A young lady is a female child who has just done something dreadful.

Judith Martin

There is a point at which you aren't
as much mum and daughter as you
are adults and friends.

JAMIE LEE CURTIS

Oh my son's my son
till he gets him a wife,
But my daughter's
my daughter all her life.

DINAH CRAIK

A busy mother makes
slothful daughters.

PROVERB

Right now, my daughter's just rolling her eyes at everything I do; I'm just an embarrassment.

ELIZABETH PERKINS

Trust not your daughters' minds by what you see them act.

WILLIAM SHAKESPEARE

I try to parent equally, but I think little girls are a little more sensitive.

DON JOHNSON

LITTLE GIRLS ARE THE NICEST THINGS THAT HAPPEN TO PEOPLE.

Alan Beck

I'm going to have to live vicariously through my daughter's rebellion because I certainly never did go through adolescence.

BROOKE SHIELDS

I keep seeing myself in my daughter, and I see my mother in me and in her. Bloody hell.

JULIE WALTERS

Your mothers get mighty shocked… nowadays, but in her day, her mother was just on the verge of sending her to reform school.

WILL ROGERS

SMELLS LIKE TEEN SPIRIT

Telling a teenager the facts of life is like giving a fish a bath.

Arnold H. Glasow

Mothers of teenagers know why
animals eat their young.

ANONYMOUS

As a parent you try to maintain a
certain amount of control and so
you have this tug of war… You
have to learn when to let go.

ARETHA FRANKLIN

Little children, headache;
big children, heartache.

PROVERB

Imagination is something that sits up with Dad and Mum the first time their teenager stays out late.

LANE OLINGHOUSE

I think it's a mother's duty to embarrass their children.

CHER

Adolescence: a stage between infancy and adultery.

AMBROSE BIERCE

ADOLESCENCE IS THE 'CONJUGATOR' OF CHILDHOOD AND ADULTHOOD.

Louise J. Kaplan

When he's thirteen, gremlins
carry him away and leave…
a stranger who gives you not
a moment's peace.

JILL EIKENBERRY ON TEENAGE SONS

HAVING A THIRTEEN-YEAR-OLD…
IS LIKE HAVING A GENERAL
ADMISSION TICKET TO THE
MOVIES, RADIO AND TV.

Max Lerner

The best way to keep children
at home is to make the home
atmosphere pleasant, and let
the air out of the tyres.

DOROTHY PARKER

'Thank God it's Monday.' If any
working mother has not
experienced that feeling, her
children are not adolescent.

ANN DIEHL

Teenagers are God's
punishment for having sex.

PATRICK MURRAY

The modern child will answer you back before you've said anything.

Laurence J. Peter

GROWING
PAINS

GROWN DON'T MEAN NOTHING TO A MOTHER.

Toni Morrison

If you've never been hated by your child, you've never been a parent.

BETTE DAVIS

If you want children to keep their feet on the ground, put some responsibility on their shoulders.

ABIGAIL VAN BUREN

The successful mother sets her children free and becomes more free herself in the process.

ROBERT J. HAVIGHURST

It kills you to see them grow up.
But I guess it would kill you
quicker if they didn't.

BARBARA KINGSOLVER

The fingerprints on the wall
appear higher and higher.
Then suddenly they disappear.

DOROTHY EVSLIN

Children begin by loving their
parents; as they grow older they
judge them; sometimes they
forgive them.

OSCAR WILDE

You see much more of your children once they leave home.

Lucille Ball

SOME
MOTHERS
DO 'AVE 'EM

I DON'T APPROVE OF SMACKING – I JUST USE A CATTLE PROD.

Jenny Eclair

Children are gleeful barbarians.

JOSEPH MORGENSTERN

Children nowadays are tyrants. They contradict their parents, gobble their food and tyrannise their teachers.

SOCRATES

If my mum reads that I'm grammatically incorrect, I'll have hell to pay.

LARISA OLEYNIK

My mother had a great deal of trouble
with me, but I think she enjoyed it.

MARK TWAIN

Kids can be a pain in the neck when
they're not a lump in your throat.

BARBARA JOHNSON

All mothers think their children
are oaks, but the world never
lacks for cabbages.

ROBERTSON DAVIES

Me? An angel! Just ask
my mum about that!

Charlotte Church

When children are doing nothing,
they are doing mischief.

HENRY FIELDING

HAVING ONE CHILD MAKES YOU
A PARENT; HAVING TWO YOU
ARE A REFEREE.

David Frost

PARENTING
101

A mother always has to think twice, once for herself and once for her child.

SOPHIA LOREN

ALWAYS HAVE A CHANGE OF SHIRT IN THE CAR — ONE THAT BLENDS WITH SPIT-UP IS A GOOD CHOICE!

Bridget Moynahan

Just do your job right and
your kids will love you.

ETHEL WATERS

If you want your children to listen,
try talking softly – to someone else.

ANN LANDERS

Parents… spend half their time
wondering how their children will
turn out, and the rest… when
they will turn in.

ELEANOR GRAHAM VANCE

With parenting, there are
no real answers.

KATE HUDSON

One motivation is worth ten threats,
two pressures and six reminders.

PAUL SWEENEY

There's no road map on how to
raise a family: it's always an
enormous negotiation.

MERYL STREEP

I JUST TAKE IT HOUR BY HOUR.

Debra Messing

Children behave as well as
they are treated.

JAN HUNT

PARENTS WHO ARE AFRAID TO PUT
THEIR FOOT DOWN USUALLY HAVE
CHILDREN WHO STEP ON THEIR TOES.

Proverb

Sing out loud in the car even,
or especially, if it embarrasses
your children.

MARILYN PENLAND

A family is a unit composed…
of children… men, women, an
occasional animal, and the
common cold.

OGDEN NASH

If you must hold yourself up to your
children… hold yourself up as a
warning and not as an example.

GEORGE BERNARD SHAW

The most consistent gift and burden of motherhood is advice.

Susan Chira

To bring up a child in the way he
should go, travel that way yourself
once in a while.

JOSH BILLINGS

Most children threaten at times to
run away from home. This is the only
thing that keeps some parents going.

PHYLLIS DILLER

Allow children to be happy in
their own way, for what better
way will they find?

SAMUEL JOHNSON

SUPERMUM

GOD COULD NOT BE EVERYWHERE, SO HE CREATED MOTHERS.

Proverb

Being a working mum is not easy.
You have to be willing to screw
up at every level.

JAMI GERTZ

Any mother could perform the
jobs of several air traffic
controllers with ease.

LISA ALTHER

If evolution really works, how come
mothers only have two hands?

MILTON BERLE

A man's work is from sun to sun,
but a mother's work is never done.

ANONYMOUS

My idea of superwoman is someone
who scrubs her own floors.

BETTE MIDLER

She never quite leaves her children
at home, even when she doesn't
take them along.

MARGARET CULKIN BANNING

To describe my mother
would be to write about
a hurricane in its
perfect power.

Maya Angelou

An ounce of mother is
worth a ton of priest.

PROVERB

I know how to do anything –
I'm a mum.

ROSEANNE BARR

I plan everything in advance…
We have charts, maps and lists on
the fridge, all over the house.
I sometimes feel like I'm
with the CIA.

KATE WINSLET

All mothers are
working mothers.

ANONYMOUS

THERE IS NO WAY TO BE A PERFECT
MOTHER, AND A MILLION WAYS TO
BE A GOOD ONE.

Jill Churchill

I'd like to sleep a tiny bit more.

KATE BECKINSALE

A MOTHER... SEEING THERE ARE
ONLY FOUR PIECES OF PIE FOR FIVE
PEOPLE, PROMPTLY ANNOUNCES SHE
NEVER DID CARE FOR PIE.

Tenneva Jordan

MOTHER
KNOWS
BEST

MOTHERS ARE INSTINCTIVE PHILOSOPHERS.

Harriet Beecher Stowe

When your mother asks, 'Do you want a piece of advice?'… You're going to get it anyway.

ERMA BOMBECK

A smart mother makes often a better diagnosis than a poor doctor.

AUGUST BIER

The hand that rocks the cradle is the hand that rules the world.

W. R. WALLACE

That best academy,
a mother's knee.

JAMES RUSSELL LOWELL

What the mother sings goes all
the way down to the coffin.

HENRY WARD BEECHER

One good mother is worth a
hundred schoolmasters.

GEORGE HERBERT

My mother was like a drill sergeant.

George W. Bush

[A] mother is one to whom you hurry when you are troubled.

EMILY DICKINSON

My mother made a brilliant impression upon my childhood life. She shone for me like the evening star.

WINSTON CHURCHILL

Find out what they want and then advise them to do it.

HARRY S. TRUMAN ON GIVING GUIDANCE TO A CHILD

If a mother could ask a fairy
godmother to endow [her child]
with the most useful gift, that
gift would be curiosity.

ELEANOR ROOSEVELT

No influence is so powerful as
that of the mother.

SARAH JOSEPHA HALE

The art of mothering is to teach
the art of living to children.

ELAINE HEFFNER

A CHILD EDUCATED ONLY AT SCHOOL IS AN UNEDUCATED CHILD.

George Santayana

I know enough to know that when
you're in a pickle… call Mum.

JENNIFER GARNER

Even a secret agent can't lie
to a Jewish mother.

PETER MALKIN

Mothers always know.

OPRAH WINFREY

WE'RE ALL GOING ON A SUMMER HOLIDAY

Mothers... They are the 'vacationless' class.

Anne Morrow Lindbergh

Babies don't need a vacation, but I still see them at the beach.

STEVEN WRIGHT

A HOLIDAY IS WHEN THE FAMILY GOES AWAY FOR A REST, ACCOMPANIED BY A MOTHER WHO SEES THAT THE OTHERS GET IT.

Marcelene Cox

Outings are so much more fun when we can savour them through the children's eyes.

LAWANA BLACKWELL

In America there are two classes of travel – first class, and with children.

ROBERT BENCHLEY

Honolulu, it's got everything. Sand for the children, sun for the wife, sharks for the wife's mother.

KEN DODD

NOBODY PUTS BABY IN THE CORNER

Sweater, n. Garment worn by child
when its mother is feeling chilly.

AMBROSE BIERCE

There is nothing like becoming a
mum to fill you with fear.

ARIANNA HUFFINGTON

If the kids are still alive when my
husband gets home… then, hey,
I've done my job.

ROSEANNE BARR

The watchful mother tarries nigh,
though sleep has closed her
infant's eyes.

JOHN KEBLE

There's some sort of mother blood
that just wants you to buy firearms
when you have a child.

COURTNEY LOVE

Children tell you casually years later
what it would have killed you with
worry to know at the time.

MIGNON McLAUGHLIN

No one understands my ills,
nor the terror that fills my breast,
who does not know the
heart of a mother.

MARIE ANTOINETTE

AS A MUM, I ALWAYS FEEL I HAVE
TO PROTECT THEM.

Jami Gertz on her children

GRANDMA, WE LOVE YOU

If nothing is going well, call
your grandmother.

PROVERB

Why do grandparents
and grandchildren get along
so well? They have the same
enemy – the mother.

CLAUDETTE COLBERT

Are we not like two volumes of
one book?

MARCELINE DESBORDES-VALMORE ON THE
RELATIONSHIP BETWEEN PARENTS AND GRANDPARENTS

IT IS AS GRANDMOTHERS THAT OUR MOTHERS COME INTO THE FULLNESS OF THEIR GRACE.

Christopher Morley

It's such a grand thing to be a mother of a mother – that's why the world calls her grandmother.

ANONYMOUS

YOUR SONS WEREN'T MADE TO LIKE YOU. THAT'S WHAT GRANDCHILDREN ARE FOR.

Jane Smiley

Just about the time
a woman thinks
her work is done, she
becomes a grandmother.

Edward H. Dreschnack

Grandmother – a wonderful
mother with lots of practice.

ANONYMOUS

Few things are more satisfying
than seeing your children have
teenagers of their own.

DOUG LARSON

Most grandmas have a touch
of the scallywag.

HELEN THOMSON

Never have children,
only grandchildren.

GORE VIDAL

If your baby is 'beautiful and…
an angel all the time', you're
the grandma.

TERESA BLOOMINGDALE

Being pretty on the inside means
you don't hit your brother and you
eat all your peas – that's what my
grandma taught me.

LORD CHESTERFIELD

MAN
ABOUT THE
HOUSE

MY MOTHER BURIED THREE HUSBANDS, AND TWO OF THEM WERE JUST NAPPING.

Rita Rudner

The most important thing a father can do for his children is to love their mother.

THEODORE HESBURGH

Watching your husband become a father is really sexy and wonderful.

CINDY CRAWFORD

Babies don't need fathers, but mothers do. Someone who is taking care of a baby needs to be taken care of.

AMY HECKERLING

Kids learn by example. If I respect
Mum, they're going to respect Mum.

TIM ALLEN

Like all parents, my husband
and I just do the best we can, and
hold our breath, and hope we've set
aside enough money to pay for
our kids' therapy.

MICHELLE PFEIFFER

The purpose of my life is being
a father to my kids and being a
husband to my wife.

TERRENCE HOWARD

No man is responsible
for his father. That was
entirely his mother's affair.

Margaret Turnbull

FATHERS SHOULD BE NEITHER SEEN NOR HEARD. THAT IS THE ONLY PROPER BASIS FOR FAMILY LIFE.

Oscar Wilde

Mothers are fonder than fathers
of their children because they are
more certain they are their own.

ARISTOTLE

HAVING A BABY IS LIKE FALLING
IN LOVE AGAIN, BOTH WITH YOUR
HUSBAND AND YOUR CHILD.

Tina Brown

It really is asking too much of a woman to expect her to bring up a husband and her children too.

LILIAN BELL

All women should know how to take care of children. Most of them will have a husband some day.

FRANKLIN P. JONES

I have the advantage of having a lot of help, a real hands-on husband and small children whom I can easily manipulate.

JANE KACZMAREK

THE BIRDS
AND THE
BEES

Don't bother discussing
sex with small children.
They rarely have
anything to add.

Fran Lebowitz

It is not economical to go to
bed early to save the candles
if the result is twins.

PROVERB

CHILDREN ALWAYS ASSUME THE
SEXUAL LIVES OF THEIR PARENTS
COME TO A GRINDING HALT AT
THEIR CONCEPTION.

Alan Bennett

Parenthood: the state of being better chaperoned than you were before marriage.

MARCELENE COX

The most effective form of birth control I know is spending the day with my kids.

JILL BENSLEY

While we try to teach our children about life, our children teach us what life is all about.

ANGELA SCHWINDT

I'M A VIRGIN AND I BROUGHT UP ALL MY CHILDREN TO BE THE SAME.

Shirley Bassey

HEIR-
RAISING
EXPERIENCES

Our mothers always remain the strangest, craziest people we've ever met.

Marguerite Duras

I'd like to be the ideal mother,
but I'm too busy raising my kids.

ANONYMOUS

I feel incredibly lucky and blessed,
but I do sometimes feel like that
Exorcist lady!

KATE BECKINSALE

Tired mothers find that spanking
takes less time than reasoning and
penetrates sooner to the
seat of the memory.

WILL DURANT

If there were no schools to take the
children away from home…
the insane asylums would be
filled with mothers.

E. W. HOWE

The mother – poor invaded soul –
finds even the bathroom door no
bar to hammering little hands.

CHARLOTTE PERKINS GILMAN

Mothers are all slightly insane.

J. D. SALINGER

WITH TWO SMALL CHILDREN... THE CHANCE TO GO SHOPPING IS WAY DOWN THE LIST.

Jo Brand

The lullaby is the spell whereby
the mother attempts to transform
herself back from an ogre to a saint.

JAMES FENTON

Raising a kid is part joy and
part guerilla warfare.

ED ASNER

Tranquilisers work only if you
follow the advice on the bottle –
keep away from children.

PHYLLIS DILLER

FAIREST OF THEM ALL

As long as a woman can look ten years younger than her own daughter, she is perfectly satisfied.

Oscar Wilde

SHE'S THE EPITOME OF BEAUTY... BUT SHE IS A BEAUTIFUL MOTHER, TOO.

Kate Hudson on her mother Goldie Hawn

Thou art thy mother's glass,
and she in thee calls back the
lovely April of her prime.

WILLIAM SHAKESPEARE

MOTHERHOOD HAS A VERY
HUMANISING EFFECT. EVERYTHING
GETS REDUCED TO ESSENTIALS.

Meryl Streep

I got my figure back after giving birth. Sad, I'd hoped to get somebody else's.

CAROLINE QUENTIN

I STILL LOVE CLOTHES... BUT FOR EVERYDAY, IT WOULD BE FOOLISH TO SPEND MORE TIME ON MY OUTFIT THAN I DO ON MY SON.

Sarah Jessica Parker

GETTING OLD

Be nice to your children because they are the ones who will choose your rest home.

Phyllis Diller

I refuse to admit that I am more
than fifty-two, even if that does
make my sons illegitimate.

NANCY ASTOR

The woman who tells her age is either
too young to have anything to lose or
too old to have anything to gain.

PROVERB

A homely face and no figure
have aided many women
heavenward.

MINNA ANTRIM

There are only two things a child
will share willingly: communicable
diseases and its mother's age.

BENJAMIN SPOCK

Children are a great comfort in your
old age – and they help you
reach it faster, too.

LIONEL KAUFFMAN

I believe the sign of maturity is
accepting deferred gratification.

PEGGY CAHN

WRINKLES ARE HEREDITARY – PARENTS GET THEM FROM THEIR CHILDREN.

Doris Day

JUST LIKE MAMA USED TO MAKE

My children won't eat my food. If it is not plastic or out of a box, then they are not interested.

Nigella Lawson

There are times when parenthood seems nothing but feeding the mouth that bites you.

PETER DE VRIES

For thirty years she served the family nothing but leftovers. The original meal has never been found.

CALVIN TRILLIN

My mother's menu consisted of two choices: take it or leave it.

BUDDY HACKETT

Hot dogs always seem better out than at home… so do your children.

MIGNON McLAUGHLIN

My cooking is so bad my kids thought Thanksgiving was to commemorate Pearl Harbour.

PHYLLIS DILLER

Children should come to the table clean and in a merry mood.

ERASMUS

I WAS BORN BECAUSE
MY MOTHER NEEDED
A FOURTH FOR MEALS.

Beatrice Lillie

Govern a family as you would cook
a small fish – very gently.

PROVERB

Raising children is like making
biscuits… raise a big batch as one,
while you have your hands
in the dough.

E. W. HOWE

If God had intended us to follow
recipes, he wouldn't have given
us grandmothers.

LINDA HENLEY

IT'S ALL
ABOUT THE
MUMMY

I thought my mum's whole purpose was to be my mum. That's how she made me feel.

NATASHA GREGSON WAGNER

MY MOTHER COULD MAKE ANYBODY FEEL GUILTY – SHE USED TO GET LETTERS OF APOLOGY FROM PEOPLE SHE DIDN'T EVEN KNOW.

Joan Rivers

Of all the rights of
women, the greatest is
to be a mother.

Lin Yutang

A mother understands what
a child does not say.

PROVERB

Mother – that was the bank where we
deposited all our hurts and worries.

THOMAS DE WITT TALMAGE

A Freudian slip is when you say one
thing but mean your mother.

ANONYMOUS

MOTHER IS THE ONE WE COUNT ON FOR THE THINGS THAT MATTER MOST OF ALL.

Katharine Butler Hathaway

A mother's arms are made of tenderness and children sleep soundly in them.

VICTOR HUGO

A mother is not a person to lean on, but a person to make leaning unnecessary.

DOROTHY CANFIELD FISHER

A mother's love for her child is like nothing else in the world.

AGATHA CHRISTIE

WHAT'S THE
GOOD OF
CHILDREN?

Having children gives
your life purpose. Right
now, my purpose is to
get some sleep.

Reno Goodale

Adults are always asking little kids
what they want to be when they grow
up because they're looking for ideas.

PAULA POUNDSTONE

Children… are like flowers in
a bouquet: there's always one
determined to face in an
opposite direction.

MARCELENE COX

I said I would get better with
each baby, and I have.

DEMI MOORE

Children are the only form of
immortality that we can be sure of.

PETER USTINOV

Only mothers can think of the
future – because they give birth
to it in their children.

MAXIM GORKY

Children are the anchors that
hold a mother to life.

SOPHOCLES

YOU WILL ALWAYS BE YOUR CHILD'S FAVOURITE TOY.

Vicki Lansky

MUMMY, DEAREST

No language can
express the power and
beauty and heroism
of a mother's love.

Edwin H. Chapin

The greatest love is a mother's, then
a dog's, then a sweetheart's.

PROVERB

All motherly love is really without
reason and logic.

JOAN CHEN

Motherhood is not for the faint-
hearted. Frogs, skinned knees, and
the insults of teenage girls are not
meant for the wimpy.

DANIELLE STEEL

Heaven is at the feet of mothers.

PROVERB

Mama exhorted… 'jump at de sun'.
We might not land on the sun, but at
least we would get off the ground.

ZORA NEALE HURSTON

Youth fades; love droops; the leaves
of friendship fall; A mother's secret
hope outlives them all.

OLIVER WENDELL HOLMES

A MOTHER'S LOVE PERCEIVES NO IMPOSSIBILITIES.

Cornelia Paddock

OUR
HOUSE

I am a marvellous housekeeper. Every time I leave a man I keep his house.

Zsa Zsa Gabor

Everybody wants to save the earth;
nobody wants to help Mum
with the dishes.

P. J. O'ROURKE

Housework is what a woman does
that nobody notices unless she
hasn't done it.

EVAN ESAR

Children really brighten up a
household. They never turn
the lights off.

RALPH BUS

If you worked hard and prospered, someone else would do it for you.

NORA EPHRON ON HER MOTHER'S BELIEF ABOUT COOKING

YOU CAN'T CONTROL THINGS LIKE YOU USED TO... I LIKE TO KEEP THINGS VERY CLEAN, BUT ALL THAT GOES OUT THE WINDOW!

Kerri Russell

TEENAGERS WHO ARE NEVER REQUIRED TO VACUUM ARE LIVING IN ONE.

Fred G. Gosman

The interesting thing about being a mother is that everyone wants pets, but no one but me cleans the kitty litter.

MERYL STREEP

They're all mine… Of course, I'd trade any of them for a dishwasher.

ROSEANNE BARR ON HER CHILDREN

What is a home without children? Quiet.

HENNY YOUNGMAN

PUSHY
MUMS

No matter how old a mother is, she watches her middle-aged children for signs of improvement.

Florida Scott-Maxwell

I doubt if a charging elephant, or a rhino, is as determined or hard to check as a socially ambitious mother.

WILL ROGERS

My mother was against me being an actress – until I introduced her to Frank Sinatra.

ANGIE DICKINSON

It is quite surprising how many children survive in spite of their mothers.

NORMAN DOUGLAS

A GOOD EDUCATION IS THE NEXT BEST THING TO A PUSHY MOTHER.

Charles Schultz

MOTHER ALWAYS SAID

My mother said to me, 'If you are a soldier, you will become a general…' Instead, I was a painter, and became Picasso.

PABLO PICASSO

My mum always said that there would be haters. Not everyone can love ya.

JOEL MADDEN

My mum always says, 'You make your own luck.'

ORLANDO BLOOM

My mum used to say that Greek
Easter was later because then you
get stuff cheaper.

AMY SEDARIS

My mother used to say, 'He who
angers you, conquers you!' But my
mother was a saint.

ELIZABETH KENNY

Mum always tells me to celebrate
everyone's uniqueness.

HILARY DUFF

She would tell me Adam was the rough draft and Eve was the final product.

Daphne Zuniga

MY MUM SAID THE ONLY REASON MEN ARE ALIVE IS FOR LAWN CARE AND VEHICLE MAINTENANCE.

Tim Allen

My mum is always telling me it takes
a long time to get to the top, but a
short time to get to the bottom.

MILEY CYRUS

Mother told me to be good but
she's been wrong before.

ANONYMOUS

She said, 'You may be pretty, and you
may be talented, but nobody will
remember that if you're mean.'

KATIE HOLMES ON HER MUM'S BEAUTY ADVICE

MUM'S THE WORD

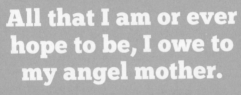

All that I am or ever hope to be, I owe to my angel mother.

Abraham Lincoln

Mothers are a biological necessity;
fathers are a social invention.

MARGARET MEAD

I couldn't live without my music,
man. Or me mum.

ROBBIE WILLIAMS

She was… hated at tea parties,
feared in shops, and loved at crises.

THOMAS HARDY ON HIS MOTHER

God could not be everywhere,
and therefore he made mothers.

RUDYARD KIPLING

MY MOTHER IS A WALKING MIRACLE.

Leonardo DiCaprio

TO A CHILD'S EAR, 'MOTHER' IS MAGIC IN ANY LANGUAGE.

Arlene Benedict

If you're interested in finding out more about our books, find us on Facebook at Summersdale Publishers and follow us on Twitter at @Summersdale.

www.summersdale.com